WAYPOINTS

poems by

Johanna DeMay

Finishing Line Press
Georgetown, Kentucky

WAYPOINTS

Copyright © 2022 by Johanna DeMay
ISBN 979-8-88838-031-4 First Edition
All rights reserved under International and Pan-American Copyright Conventions. No part of this book may be reproduced in any manner whatsoever without written permission from the publisher, except in the case of brief quotations embodied in critical articles and reviews.

Publisher: Leah Huete de Maines
Editor: Christen Kincaid
Cover Art: Johanna DeMay
Author Photo: Will DeMay
Cover Design: Elizabeth Maines McCleavy

Order online: www.finishinglinepress.com
also available on amazon.com

Author inquiries and mail orders:
Finishing Line Press
P. O. Box 1626
Georgetown, Kentucky 40324
U. S. A.

Table of Contents

1—POINTS OF DEPARTURE

Evidence of an Earlier Life 1
Stories.. 2
David... 4
Cliff Diver 5
Three Love Songs for Chavela Vargas...................................... 7
Postcard from Paris 10
Provenance 11
My Mother's Voice.. 12
Oral History Project... 13
The Ruins 14
Words and Music.. 16
Migration's Soundtrack.. 18

2—FLASH POINTS

Unresolved... 21
Three Citizens 22
Cycling in Indian Country 24
At Night 25
Border Town 27
Un Refrán is not a Refrain 28
Cristina's Odyssey—2019 30
No One Stays in Honduras.. 33
Variations on a Theme 36
Category V... 37
In Lockdown 38
Unraveling 39

3—BREAKING POINTS

Flashbacks 43
Testimony 45
The Derelict 48
At Low Ebb 49
What Sisters Do 50
Unhinged 52
Heartbreak 53
Unwelcome Changes 54
Waypoints 55

4—INFLECTION POINTS

No Visible Scars 59
Emily's Teacup 61
Elegy for my Vacuum Cleaner and other Artifacts 63
Biography of a Pomegranate Tree 65
English as a Second Language 67
La Patrona 69
Final Walk-Through 70
Acts of Faith 71
Applied Sciences 73
Love Locks on the Rio Grande 74
Bushcraft 76
Grace 78

*To Will, who makes all our waypoints possible,
and our children Rafael and Alexandra,
who make every waypoint meaningful.
And to Diana, keen-eyed mentor—her insightful comments
help me grow, her generosity never fails me.*

1— POINTS OF DEPARTURE

EVIDENCE OF AN EARLIER LIFE

After the shipwreck scattered belongings
washed ashore with me.
No captain's log was found, no witnesses
could confirm or contest
what I recall.

Memory
is a maze of windswept dunes.
Tides rise and fall,
erase my footprints,
level my sandcastle's walls
—leave me stranded,
cut off from homeland and tribe,
an outlier among well-meaning strangers.

I rub old scars
the way a blind woman fingers braille,
hoard what solid evidence
still remains.

A 1950's green cashmere cardigan
cached in the family cedar chest—
proof my mother wasn't always
a heavy woman. In the margins
of a dogeared, splattered "Joy of Cooking"
—notes scribbled in her wandering script.

A tattered black and white snapshot
of the dark haired deserter whose name
I once shared—that spook who reappears
in my bathroom mirror, in my creased
forehead, my stubborn chin.

I squint to catch sight of the girl I was.
The grandmother I've become
meets my gaze, shrugs.

STORIES

Adults loomed over me
like trees, their distant faces
blurred. They scooped me up,
took me away, never said

where we were going.
Nameless strangers
told me not to worry,
promised they'd take care of me.

But I knew what I knew,
gave answers before
I heard the questions.
I was an angry child.

A doll-faced girl in a ruffled dress
pointed to a skywriter overhead.
*Look! God's finger's inside the plane
writing letters on the sky!*

God?
I laughed at her silly story.
*There is no God.
It's an airplane and some smoke.*
Weeping, she fled to her mother.

Mine scolded me—didn't say
I was wrong—just told me
I should try not to upset
the neighbors.

Did she mean I should put other people's
feelings first—or hide my own?
I saw no sign of God the Father, All Powerful,
All Knowing, loving and just. In my world

father was a broken promise. Defiant,
I stood on my own small feet. Vigilant,
I slept little, eyes wide and ears alert
to any movement in the night.

Grownups lit candles in the dark,
made up unlikely stories meant
to comfort. I did not believe,
but learned to value kindness.

DAVID

From birth he turned his head away,
refused our mother's breast, arched
his tiny back, writhed, punched, wailed.
She could not comfort him.

She laid him in his crib, pressed his bottle
into my four-year-old hands, numbed
her grief with Phenobarbital.
I could not comfort her.

When I sang my made-up lullabies
David's little fists uncurled.
He suckled—never smiled—
but as long as I was near he didn't cry.

My brother learned to walk—not to speak.
Music was his mother tongue—he hummed
snatches of "Eine Kleine Nachtmusik,"
"Peter and the Wolf." We sang pitch-perfect
harmonies—had no need of words.

He was six, I was ten, when Mother left him
in a state asylum. For years she mourned
in her darkened room. I wept alone in mine.
We never said his name.

When I turned twenty-one I searched for him.
Rockland State Hospital had been closed,
patients discharged, no records kept.
Nobody knew where my brother went.

When asked I say
I was an only child.
I have a son. I did not
name him David.

CLIFF DIVER

Backlit against a blue-gold sky,
arms raised, the diver launches
over the edge like a seagull.
He soars, pivots, folds his wings
and plummets. White toothed breakers
slam into a pocket sized slot,
shatter against sheer walls.
Streamers of spray fly at the sun.

When the wave subsides,
stone skewers break the surface
like claws unsheathed.
A dark head shoots up
through the churning foam.
The diver swims to the wall,
clings to wet scree, climbs
out and bows. I push
windblown hair from my eyes,
count heartbeats, gulp salty air.

In the lull of the backwash
a second diver takes on
the void. He times pulse,
breath and leap to the swell
of the incoming wave. *This must be
a trick, like the circus girl sawed in half.*

Next comes a boy my own age.
Coached by an elder, he starts each dive
a few steps higher up the cliff.
As he reaches toward the top of the sky
his back arches, his ribs jut out.
I tug my skinny knees to my chest.
Now it's real: terror rises from bone
marrow, rides red blood cells,
ripples through tensed veins.

The roar of sky-high waves
in a rocky cleft replays
in my nightmares still.

THREE LOVE SONGS FOR CHAVELA VARGAS

I. PRIMER AMOR

Your voice ambushed me where
I stood, caught in the doorway at the end
of childhood. Gooseflesh prickled.

You sang with the rumbling growl
of a thunderhead gnawing on craggy
ridges and wind scarred peaks.

Echoes of *La Llorona* sobbed in your voice—
poor wandering ghost, mourning the
children she loved and murdered for spite.

Your love songs throbbed
with the rhythm and power
of your pulse. The heat

of your desire unhinged me.
I was marked for life by the hoarse
urgency of your voice.

II. AMOR DE MI VIDA

Who were you, Chavela? What
gave you the courage to stride
through the barbed wire barriers

of unshakable macho rule? You challenged
them all, a woman wearing the pants of a peasant,
poor but armed with a guitar and a gun.

The Plaza Garibaldi surrendered to you.
The headwaters of mariachi music
and turbulent rivers of tequila were yours.

In the cantinas and on the street, you wept
for Mexico's sorrows...and your own.
Desolation, rage, the bitter backlash

of abduction and rape, all the Conquest's
orphans and bastards howled with you
down unlit alleys and twisted cobblestoned streets.

But under the blood red *jorongo* slung
over your shoulders—banner and shield—
your heart was never hidden.

A stubborn tenderness seeped
into your angriest lyrics. Love and joy
whispered in your darkest notes.

III. MI ULTIMO AMOR

When I left home your voice came with me:
"*¡No te rajes!* Hold nothing back! Be fearless.
Be a woman—*¡una mujer muy mujer!*"

While I grew stronger, despair unraveled you.
Tequila dragged you over the edge of blindness
and drowned your voice. Only the echo lingered.

Nameless and homeless, sheltered
by strangers, you faded off
into legend...but did not die.

You came back sober. Your voice
was cracked but your heart
was a drum—it went on pounding.

You came back singing: "*Ya solo
me quedan ganas de acostarme
en el regazo de la muerte.*"

In the end, all you longed for was
to lie down in death's lap....
"También eso será hermoso."

Your voice is gone now but your words linger:
"Remember me as you like. Just say what you feel.
Say what you lived with me."

Chavela, you taught me to live.
Only you could teach me at last
to embrace my own death like a lover.

POSTCARD FROM PARIS

She stepped in front of me,
a scrawny child, shawl wound
tight against the wind, curly hair
run amok, freckles, green eyes
behind a mask of black makeup.

A postcard of a much younger me.

Is this your first visit to Paris?
…smooth as a tour guide
greeting a guest.

Lo siento, no hablo inglés.

She switched into sing-song Spanish,
a chameleon changing color.
I'm hungry. Give me a little coin.

My stomach clenched,
concrete underfoot turned to sand.

*I'm pregnant. See, my baby
is growing. Just give me
something to feed him.*

I remembered the sting
when strangers shook their heads
at my swollen belly.

She stared at me like a stray cat
stranded in rush hour traffic.
Would she pocket my paltry gift
and saunter off to a waiting Mercedes?

Purse clamped to my side,
I bolted. Now the thought of her
aches like a broken bone.

PROVENANCE

At a time when large families crammed
into small houses, wore patched coats,
darned socks, hand-me-down boots,

Great grandfather paid for craftsmanship—solid oak,
sober lines, joints built to last. Faint rings map
where his coffee mug perched, scorch marks

where cigarettes smoldered as he read
about breadlines, dust-storms, foreclosures,
ragtag caravans of overloaded jalopies headed west.

While the coal furnace clanked in the cellar
he hunkered down in his rocker—maimed
railroad-man hobbled by a wooden leg,

cast aside like a shattered wheel. Without him
Great-grandmother shriveled—lone apple
on a bare branch, longing for a winter storm

to knock her down. We never met, yet at times
I sense the old man's tight-lipped presence,
Post-Gazette spread across his lap.

I tape an index card under the tattered seat:
Mission Style Rocking Chair, c. 1914.
Belonged to Great grandfather John.

MY MOTHER'S VOICE

It's October again and the cranes
are returning. They filled the sky
the day I learned of your death.
I did not cry. Over time I've grown
used to your absence, a lost limb
that no longer throbs.

A wary child, I watched you
the way sailors study the weather.
On good days your love songs
soared through our upstairs windows,
made passing strangers smile.
I savored your joy like a morsel
of dark chocolate, knowing
it would not last. Barricaded
inside your bedroom,
you burrowed under blankets
and wept. Crouched outside
your door, I wept with you.

Why has today's tsunami of wings
triggered such tears?
You've followed me, whispered
in the long hallways of my bones.
Now you are silent,
a piano without strings.

ORAL HISTORY PROJECT

Fingers arched over his keyboard,
my eleven-year-old grandson
calls me to the kitchen table.

Where were you born? When? Family name?
Hebrew name? Which relative came here first?
Why?

My father—just 14—ran away from Vitepsk
to join the Russian Army, fight in the Great War.
They turned him away. He had hammertoes.

Spiked eyebrows punctuate Caleb's
surprise, like before & after
question marks in Spanish.

Yes, "hidden toes" just like yours.
With ordinary toes he might've become
a soldier, died on a frozen battle field.

My grandson glances at his bare feet.
What's your favorite memory of him?

When we crossed the bay to Roqueta
in a motorboat, he swam across. My mother
muttered about riptides, jellyfish, sharks.

Playful as a seal, he plunged past breakers,
rose from the water like a shimmering merman,
bellowed, *I'm hungry, let's eat!*

Caleb presses clenched fists to his mouth.
What made your father so brave?
I shrug, *He survived a pogrom.*

How do you spell pogrom?

THE RUINS

Weathered by snows
of a thousand winters,
pummeled by winds
of a thousand springs,

the walls brook my fingertips
probing old scars, unhealed
wounds. I seek traces of life.
They guard their secrets.

Spirits flicker at the edge of sight.
They call me and I come
like a pilgrim to a shrine,
a supplicant to an oracle.

No doorways pierce
the bulwarks by the cliffs
—roofless now, beams riven,
upper stories ravaged.

Their shapes mirror the mesas,
buttes and canyon walls.
Their colors mime the desert.
Sunlight floods in unhindered.

High windows frame squares of sky
blue as unrequited love, clouds
like marble and mother of pearl
that shed no rain, no mercy.

I trace stones chosen for color
and shape, placed with an eye
for pattern and precision…
or perhaps simply for strength.

Ghost builders tug at my sleeves.
Just the wind? I listen for voices,
hear my own questions… yet our hands
seem to touch through the stones.

WORDS & MUSIC

Faint at first, the lead soprano's voice
swells. Her rhythm quickens—

      staccato yips, sustained yowls—
      a piercing pre-dawn reveille.

Back-up singers blend rumbling base notes
to power the choir's crescendo.

      They're so near I sense padded paws circling
      my tent. When I raise my head, nylon rustles.

Did they hear it? I hold my breath, eavesdrop
on fast-paced conversations in a foreign tongue.

      Clear phrases, pointed questions,
      forceful answers—a passionate exchange,

purposeful, complex. What are they saying?
What life & death dramas unfold

      inside deep burrows, in treetops,
      on crumbling scree slopes

—as alien to my pampered city life
as if they played out on a different planet.

      In this dark domain, teeming
      with tiny sleepless eyes, coyotes rule.

Life-long insomniac, native-born
citizen of the blue-black night,

      I may not understand the words
      of their wild anthem, but I recognize

the coyotes' joyful music—throbbing
rhythms, jazzy riffs, soaring high notes.

    Quickened, my taut nerves hum
    liked a plucked harp.

MIGRATION'S SOUNDTRACK

Low-flying scouts arrive first—alp-horn necks,
vocal cords taut as double bass strings,
complex vocabulary—purrs, warbles, honks, trills.

Galvanized steel on my pitched roof vibrates,
amplifies their chatter. Synapses quickened,
I head out, field glasses in hand.

Lookouts circle, debate, appoint air traffic
controllers to direct incoming flocks. A loose
calligraphy of V's and W's scrawls lyrics

to migration's soundtrack—call & response perfected
mid-air between Mexico and Siberia. Pueblo peoples
call them Spirit-birds, messengers from Beyond.

For ten million years they've flown this route,
rattled mesas, canyons, mountain passes with keening,
followed braided rivers—blue lines on migration's map.

Now scarce water's dammed, diverted,
wetlands drained, shriveled to slimy ponds.
At sundown cranes throng silt-clogged canals,

scatter at dawn to glean grain from harvested fields,
court life-partners, bow to each other after they mate.
They'll dance, sing duets, take turns to brood

speckled eggs, forage for wobbly hatchlings,
guide half-grown youngsters til they know the way.
If one's lost, the survivor wails, searches, grieves.

Root-bound on my dwindling river's bank,
I glimpse crimson eye patches, pearly feathers,
detect rustling wingbeats—a choir of ghosts.

2—FLASH POINTS

UNRESOLVED

If I'd stayed rooted where I was born, never tasted
mole poblano, mangos, chirimoyas, never seen
a snow-covered volcano belch fire, ash, smoke—

never heard Chavela Vargas sing—
if I'd learned only one language,
who would I be?

Unsettled by the six-pointed star I wore, my neighbor
Carmen fingered her gold cross. Her word for "human"
was *cristiano*. At her family's table I learned

a different etiquette—they ate with their hands, shared
what they had—refried beans, tortillas. At dinnertime
an American playmate's well-to-do parents sent me home.

On Roqueta Beach, pint-sized Aída sold Chiclets, packets
of spicy *pepitas*. Cat-like, she side-stepped oily sunbathers
sizzling like prawns on the grill—taught me

even a red-haired *gringa* could slip off unseen
with the right body-language. We hiked uphill
to her one-room house—tin roof, dirt floor, mud bricks.

Twin hammocks, plank table—brown earthenware bowls,
mugs, kerosene lantern. On the floor—blackened
skillet, *comal*, soot-stained *brasero*.

An alien in my country of origin
—unlikely as a beaver in the Gobi Desert—
I do my best to blend in, lock my gate at night,

eat with fork, spoon, knife, greet neighbors
in flawless English. The identity question
remains unresolved.

THREE CITIZENS

In our Bicentennial Year my French-born
neighbor became an American. Since then
her passport has reaped a rainbow

of visas: Greece, Turkey, Egypt,
Morocco, most of Europe, a chain
of exotic Southeast Asian nations.

Toast-brown, with an eagle's profile
bequeathed by Armenian ancestors,
her appearance makes her suspect.

She enters the X-Ray booth
to prove her loose black dress hides
only her proud bosom and solid belly.

I think of my brown skinned son, born
south of the border. Between flights
on his way home from school

he sidestepped behind a pillar
as a brace of security agents
race-walked past him

tracking a fresh scent, their unseen
quarry close by. Rafael noted
their ex-football players' brawn,

how their dark suits bulged at the seams,
rehearsed his best South Texas twang,
resolved never to fly back and forth

without a copy of his citizenship papers
stashed in his wallet. And me?
I go to theaters, chat at crowded cafés,

buy holiday gifts at bustling brick & mortar
boutiques, invisible in my whiteness,
no yellow star stitched to my dress.

CYCLING IN INDIAN COUNTRY

Even by day, the Rez harbors more ghosts
than people. Seabed gone dry, the desert hints
at fire and blood. Bald headlands, sheer buttes,
sandblasted turrets—nothing thrives here

but insects, reptiles, voles, predators.
Parched plants wear armor, wield knives.
Where upthrust rock meets sky, Acoma Pueblo
stands watch at the mesa's edge.

I come to breathe light, drink distances.
History ricochets through red canyons—
thrum of hoofbeats, rumbling carts, clang
of swords, gunfire's roar. Unnerved, I pedal

into a headwind on crumbling roads,
arms braced against my wheel's judder.
Like rippling silk, mirages beckon.
The wind keens in my ears.

Mission churches mark the path of steel-clad
marauders who seized water and land,
shackled slaves, hacked off limbs, built
scaffolds. Flocks of ravens grew fat.

At a crossroads I halt, weigh the stakes
of a wrong turn. A battered rez-truck brakes,
a woman asks, *Are you OK? Do you need help?*
Yes, turn left here. No, not far. Stay safe.

Hawks hover and bob, at home
in the heartless blue. Summer clouds
voluptuous as Renaissance nudes
lollygag on the horizon.

AT NIGHT

every window gapes wide,
prays for a hint of breeze, a touch
of grace. Hears only the sawing

of crickets, one wing
rasping over another—
rushing rivers of sound.

In pre-dawn darkness
tiny stars glint like a fistful
of tossed sequins.

When sleep rejects me, Night
lures me outside, folds me
into its arms. As a child I lay

face up on the grass, drank starlight
fizzy as forbidden champagne.
Taut nerves quavered in harmony

with a choir of love-drunk cicadas.
Spun-sugar galaxies thrummed
to the same rhythm. Now strobe lights

skewer night skies. Airplanes,
satellites, helicopters stitch horizons
into a grid of glittering flyways.

Yet even blurred, widely scattered,
washed out, each silver dot signals
news of its birth, its death. At night

I close the blinds, take off my watch.
The garden's been watered. No one needs
feeding, nothing needs fixing. All I can do now

is look inward—face my foreshortened
future, my ravaged planet's heartbreak—
cup our twin flames with both palms.

BORDER TOWN

Ciudad Juárez & El Paso simmer
in a brew spiced with sibling rivalry
and desert heat. Country crooners
and *mariachi* bands arm-wrestle
for sovereignty over the airwaves,
sing siren songs to lure one another
across the line.

They sway to each other's rhythms,
swallow each other's words.
La riata becomes "lariat."
"Green grow the lilacs"
morphs into *gringos*, blue eyed
foreigners with pink skin
and straw colored hair.

In Juarez a sixth grade teacher
lectures on the 1910 Revolution.
Fingers drumming the desktop, his star student
dreams of climbing the fence beside I-10,
thumbing a ride to LA. A neighborhood
pusher loiters outside, baggies stuffed
in front pockets, pistol stashed behind.

On a day-trip I stop at an outdoor café.
An old street singer serenades me,
hands calloused, fingernails
blackened, cracked guitar weathered
as a cheap kitchen chair
left too long in the sun.
But it still makes music.

Church bells chime, loudspeakers bray,
teenagers head-butt soccer balls.
In tin cans nailed to adobe walls, geraniums
bloom hope-bright. A two thousand mile-long
jagged wound, numbed with narcotics, sutured
with steel mesh and barbed wire, the border festers.

UN REFRAN IS NOT A REFRAIN

False cognates lead us astray—
        te quiero doesn't mean *I want you*,
although sometimes it may.

Occasionally men feel embarrassed
        —a pregnant woman is *embarazada*.
Un refrán is a proverb, not a refrain.

Like my ESL students, I was born
        in one country, raised in another.
We shuttle between languages,

decipher cultural cues, determined
        to demolish the language barrier,
build a bilingual bridge over the rubble.

Alicia quotes a *refrán: El que no vive para servir,*
        no sirve para vivir. My clumsy translations flounder.
"Whomever doesn't live to serve...

isn't...? doesn't...? can't...?"
        In English a broken watch doesn't *work*,
in French it doesn't *walk*, in Spanish it doesn't *serve*.

Carlos objects, *¿Porqué?* I shrug.
        Languages are quirky, illogical
like the human minds that invent them.

Online bilingual dictionaries offer farfetched
        synonyms. I select fit—*adjective/verb/noun*—
versatile as a Swiss Army knife, fit for every task.

No sirve—useless, incompetent, unfit.
        Whomever does not live to serve, is unfit to live.
A rapier proverb, no less ruthless in English—

fitting rebuke to the Gospel of Greed, the Cult
    of Rugged Individualism, the Creed
of Me First, the Dogma of Might Makes Right.

CRISTINA'S ODYSSEY, 2019

I—CRISTINA IN EXILE

He denounces me during his sermon—
Devil, blasphemer, disgusting deviant
—a stain on our Christian community.

Thugs stalk me, chase me with bats,
threaten me with *machetes*, with guns.
¡Te van a matar! my sister warns. *Run!*

She packs tortillas, rice & beans. Hangs *abuelita's*
gold cross around my neck. In San Cristóbal
a pack of street kids tackles me, snatches it.

Over 2,500 kilometers from San Salvador to Tijuana
—bloody toes, blistered heels. At roadside *descansos*
for the fallen, plastic flowers droop in desert heat.

I dodge *narcos*, pimps, cops on the take,
wake stiff-necked, hungry, scared, in rat-infested
alleys, drafty bus stations, construction sites.

Barely-healed, a knife-wound throbs,
nerve damage ricochets through my body
—echoes that refuse to die. Broken bones knit,

never as strong. My right knee catches
like a rusty hinge when it rains. At the border
I turn myself in, appeal for asylum.

They herd me onto a plane in handcuffs
with six brown-skinned women like me.
My first flight—baptism of terror.

English batters my eardrums—surf pounding
rocks. Covert glances sting. I study my hands,
pick at grime lodged under my fingernails.

II—CRISTINA IN DETENTION

Five months in a private prison
for transgenders—concrete walls,
windowless cells, no sunlight, no color.

Huddled under an aluminum blanket
I battle fevers, chills. Vile food. I gag,
go hungry. One cup at a time,

I scoop water from tanks behind toilets.
No medicine for diarrhea, no aspirin,
no band aids. Guards answer complaints

with curses, swing batons.
Tempers flare in the bathrooms,
turf wars explode in the mess.

An ex-soldier from Nicaragua punches me—
¡Pinche puta! ¡Salvadoreña de mierda!
Will HIV kill me first, or will she?

When my *tío* sponsors me, I'm released
on parole. *Primos* pitch in for airfare,
a raincoat, a phone. A volunteer named Jean

drives me to the airport, presents her US passport,
receives a one-day "companion's pass."
Spread-eagled inside the scanner, I hold my breath.

While Jean waits, latex-gloved fingers slide
under my belt, circle my thighs. A Spanish-speaking
Security officer unzips my carry-on, rummages

skirts, blouses, sandals from Thrift-Mart.
Confiscates an eight ounce bottle of shampoo.
Wands my upturned hands, probes my purse.

No trace of gunpowder. She zips my bags shut,
straightens my scarf, wishes me *Buena suerte.*
Dry-mouthed, I mumble a feeble *Gracias.*

III—CRISTINA ON PAROLE

On our way to gate B-8, I trail my companion
past busy cafés, gaudy souvenir shops,
zigzag across the concourse toward a display

of Mexican pottery—colors vibrant
like my mother's geraniums. Jean grows irises,
hollyhocks, day lilies hardy as weeds.

My flight's delayed. Over tepid coffee we share
family photos, up-beat talk of my future.
I'll work, study English, earn a degree

in International Business. *Show them
what a transgender woman can do.*
Jean wishes her grandson could meet me.

Called for early boarding, we bypass
the queue. Jean hugs me, plants a kiss
on my sweaty cheek. *¡Mucha suerte, chica!*

If my appeal's denied they'll deport me.
We've both seen reports on *Univisión:
Returned Transgenders Murdered by Gangs.*

In the jetway I stumble, glance back. Jean signals
thumbs-up. I steady my wobbling carry-on,
walk toward the plane's open door.

NO ONE STAYS IN HONDURAS

I—ESTRELLA'S ASSAULT

San Pedro Sula, Honduras, Murder Capital
of the World. Deadly as feral dogs, *mareros**
hack off my hair— handy rope to throttle me.

Threaten to rape me with the barrel of a gun.
Laugh at my screams. The bullet wound
in my right thigh still throbs.

Twin catastrophes—civil war, Hurricane Mitch.
Narcos and gunrunners own the streets.
Survival choices—sell drugs, sell myself.

I board a northbound bus—Bible, red dress, photo
of *mamá* in my schoolbag. No one stays in Honduras.
At the Nogales crossing I surrender to ICE.

Six months in a holding pen for transgenders.
Inmates teach me to scrub toilets, floors, kitchen grills
for $1 an hour. I steer clear of baton-swinging guards.

* gang members

II—MARCELA'S LAMENT

My husband escaped death squads. Then Hurricane Mitch
flattened our house, buried him with our daughters
under rubble. Two older boys went North.
No one stays in Honduras.

Esteban, my last child, born too soon—see-through skin,
match-stick legs, eyes sealed like a newborn kitten's.
Tiny fists clutched my hair when he suckled.
He slept beside to me till his voice broke,

his upper lip sprouted fuzz. I caught him
in his cousin's *quinceañera* dress—
white satin, lace bodice and cuffs. He grew
his hair long, called himself Estrella.

She went to school daily, prayed every night.
In Bible class the pastor promised redemption.
When she limped home bloodied, a bullet lodged
deep in bone, I gave her my blessing to leave.

No one stays in Honduras. I wrote my brother
Raúl in Baltimore, said Esteban's coming.
Not Estrella. Now I pray every night.
Señor, por favor, protect her.

III—RAUL'S DILEMMA

No one stays in Honduras. My sister Marcela
sent news I'd rather not hear. How can I refuse
to help Esteban, orphaned in the womb?

A good boy, she says. But why is he in prison?
They won't release him unless I buy his ticket,

guarantee his good behavior, support him
while Immigration Court hears his case.
Will I be able to keep him out of trouble?

What if he's a *narco*, a *marero*? What if
he robs us, disgraces our family name…?

IV—ESTRELLA'S REVOLT

Paroled in boy's clothing, invisible as a curbside
sparrow, I creep into the women's bathroom,
tiptoe from stall to sink. Wash hands, shoulder

backpack bulging with slinky dresses, stiletto heels,
make-up kit, blond wig. If *Tío* Raúl discovers
my thrift-store finds, will he slam the door in my face?

His neighbors curse brown skinned newcomers.
Back-alley grafitti screams: *Fucking illegals!*
Murderers! Rapists! Go back where you came from!

No one goes back to Honduras.

VARIATIONS ON A THEME

Grandfather Joseph recalls his shtetl, torched
by blood-drunk Cossacks riding lather soaked
horses, rifles raised, sabers drawn.

Shimmer of moon glow on flowing water.
Grandmother Hannah croons in Yiddish,
Meine scheine meideleh, ick hab der lib…

In her wedding dress she stood on a chair
while her mother brushed and braided
her hair. She gave me her name,

her eagle's nose, never learned English,
died in 1918 of Spanish Flu. Other hands
brushed and braided my hair.

One hundred years on, a brown caravan,
another lethal virus. Nervous as hawks guarding
hatchlings, neighbors peer through closed blinds

at a crew of Mexican roofers—
battered straw hats, rattletrap truck.
Mariachi trumpets blare from its open cab.

I walk along an irrigation canal dug
by Pueblo people before *Conquistadores*
appeared on lather soaked horses, torched

villages, stole water and land, converted tribes
at musket-point, made them refugees in their homeland.
Concealed among the invaders' ranks,

Sephardic Jews on the run from the Inquisition.
My community—loose-knit fabric of Natives,
immigrants, refugees—could it unravel?

Twisted, gnarled, as somber as graveside mourners,
centenarian cottonwoods brood beside the canal.

CATEGORY FIVE

Spooked by my own footsteps, I scuttle
across lifeless streets, abandoned parking lots

—scenario for a B-grade sci-fi film.
At the Double Rainbow Café,

our neighborhood's *de facto* town square,
upended chairs crown tables. Lights-out

at my beloved Indie bookstore. Taped to the door
of the Fair Trade store—source of a Nigerian basket

for my knitting, an embroidered blouse from Oaxaca
for my neighbor—Tibetan prayer flags plead for health.

On Old Town's plaza, a pricey gallery's windows
wear plywood armor. Unmarked—even taggers shut down.

Oscillating sprinklers launch glittering arcs—life support
for patchy grass, parched trees. Debris collects under the *portal*

where Pueblo potters displayed burnished seed-jars,
Navajo jewelers sold silver bracelets, turquoise earrings.

In March vendors and tourists scattered like tin trailers
and tar-paper shacks in Hurricane Corona's path.

Headed home, I debate what to cook for dinner,
rehearse decontamination procedures: swab doorknob

with disinfectant, scrub hands under hot water
for twenty seconds, leave mask outside in the sun.

In the mine-shaft gloom of the I-40 underpass,
a mountain bike, a crammed shopping cart.

Wary eyes glint from the doorway of a make-shift tent.

IN LOCKDOWN

My life's turned into one of those Swedish art films
where nothing happens yet everything is revealed.
Cherished delusions of choice and control shrivel.

Hunkered down, our horizons shrink to the fence line
around our house. Grocery runs feel like armed forays
into enemy territory. Afloat in the aisles, Coronavirus

settles on counters, crouches on cart-handles,
hitches a ride home with us on cereal boxes,
Granny Smith apples, 6-packs of aluminum cans.

No dinner guests, no date nights, all travel plans postponed.
To distinguish today from yesterday, I tackle exotic recipes—
Indonesian Gado Gado, Biryani from Pakistan.

My husband grows a garden—daily ritual of watering,
constant weeding. When he scores a 25 lb. sack
of unbleached organic flour, I create sourdough starter,

bake crusty artisanal bread. My sister berates me
for social distancing, claims the pandemic's a hoax
concocted by Bill Gates and his ilk to take

away our freedoms, imprison us in our homes.
How many families will break apart before
the lockdown ends? How long will it take to heal?

As I walk past my neighbor's house, he bellows
Take off that goddamned mask! For weeks he hasn't
revved up his truck, backed out at 6:00 AM.

UNRAVELING

Held hostage by Covid 19, two white-haired
knitters share projects on Zoom.

Anita holds up colorful hats, matching
scarves, cabled socks, cozy mittens

for grandchildren in Denver. I show off
a stylish blue cardigan for my daughter.

We compare recent statistics—numbers
tested positive, hospitalizations, deaths.

Remember my cousin Teresa? Anita's needles pause.
She's on a ventilator. No one's allowed to visit.

I count stitches, control the yarn's tension, try to take
comfort in the feel of it, plush as my Persian cat's fur.

Creating useful things—my way to keep the what-if's
at bay. After November's election, a short-lived gush

of relief. Now rabid calls for violence trigger
nightmares archived in DNA—white-robed

Inquisitors, blood-crazed cossacks, cattle cars,
death camps, a sweat-drenched Senator bellowing,

Are you now or have you ever been a member…?
I shudder, skittish as a horse spooked by whiffs

from an arsonist's torch. *How can fellow citizens
hurt, even kill neighbors who disagree?*

Anita shrugs, *I'm a veteran, trained to kill
enemies. If racists harm my son, I'll kill them.*

Gobsmacked, I flinch. *Do you own a gun?*
A lit fuse, her voice sizzles. *Damn right I do!*

3—BREAKING POINTS

FLASHBACKS

Wisteria drapes the wall, shades
a rickety table where Marie-France
and I share pine-scented rosemary tea.
Gruff gusts hustle grey flocks overhead.
We clutch our sweaters, shoulders
hunched against April's raw breath.

She names each edible weed that sprouts
between cracked red paving stones:
mustard seed, lambs-quarters, purslane,
names taught by her mother's mother
who never smiled, survivor of the Armenian
genocide, the death march across Syria's desert.
*Grand-mère never shared childhood stories,
only her knowledge of plants.*

Her father's Huguenot forbearers
fled to a mountain village too remote
to be found, too poor to be fought over.
Beside the stone hearth a niche cupped
a plaster virgin, blue robes and paper roses
spread to conceal the family's bible.

In 1942 their wine cellar sheltered two Jews
and an anarchist—midnight comings
and goings cloaked by a wall of wisteria.
Uphill on the next rooftop, armed soldiers
stood guard. Red dots pulsed in the dark.
A toddler, Marie-France was forbidden
to enter the garden. She watched her mother
kneel between rows of tomatoes
and green-beans to probe for landmines.

My own ghosts don't wear green uniforms,
speak homegrown Midwestern English,
no trace of a foreign accent. An empty fridge,
an eviction notice, a subpoena, a crumpled front page

on the floor: ROSENBERGS EXECUTED.
Mother sobs, won't eat, can't sleep.
If she dies who will take David and me?
Is there a special orphanage for Jewish children?

TESTIMONY

(for Dr. Christine Blasey-Ford)

Anna:

The professor invited me into his office,
locked the door. Pinned against his tall bookcase,
I memorized titles—*Pilgrim's Progress,
Paradise Lost, The Faerie Queene.*
On his glossy mahogany desk,
a pair of family photographs,
an ash-tray, cut glass. His pipe
smoldered.

Beth:

Perched on my bed, Daddy squeezed
my new breasts—calloused fingers
kneaded my sore nipples.
*If you make a fuss
Mother will throw you out.*
When he left for a beer
my brothers flipped a coin
to decide who would go first.

Caroline:

My piano teacher stood behind me,
bent to place his hands over mine,
thrust his tongue into my ear.
My parents never understood
why I gave up my lessons.

Donna:

When he found me in tears
over my boyfriend's betrayal,
my biology teacher led me

to the roof, smashed his mouth
against mine—kiss like a fistful
of rocks, taste of stale beer,
cloying scent of Old Spice.
One hand clamped my neck,
the other slid under my skirt
....*to teach you*
what a real man is like.

Elaine:

Top-heavy, klutzy as a beached
elephant seal, I lurched down hallways
on mismatched legs, groped by jocks,
sideswiped by cheerleaders—Barbie Doll
bodies, toothpaste ad smiles.
Saddled with a reputation
I'd done nothing to earn,
at lunchtime I sat apart,
dropped out when I turned fifteen.

Frances:

My mother's bachelor uncle.
When he sniffed my neck, stiff nose hairs
prickled. More wiry hairs in his ears.
My brand-new panties—blue flowers,
heart-shaped leaves—tossed on the floor.
He said it was a game, made me ride horsey
on his thighs, pressed my pudgy hands
around his cock—pink, rubbery
as a boiled hot dog.

Helen and Irene:

After Dad died, my kid sister
and I thumbed the family album—
faded snapshots, tattered pages.
Paunchy men in white undershirts

and plaid shorts, housewives
in shapeless dresses, forties hairstyles.
No names, no dates. Our memories blank
between the ages of seven and fourteen.

Dr. Jeanne, PhD:

In a whiskey-fueled rage
he fractured my mother's jaw,
raped her when she tried to run.

After my sister's suicide
I saw her naked body—
bruises plum-purple on breasts,
belly, buttocks, thighs.

I've compiled case studies, published
research, counseled traumatized
patients—each one certain she
was somehow to blame.

THE DERELICT

He sprints to the center lane, taunts
mid-morning traffic. Stick figure
draped in a torn black T-shirt,
stork legs in frayed denim.

His arms flap—flimsy wings
too feeble to fly. He teeters, tap dances
on wobbly feet. Panicked drivers
swerve into high-speed lanes.

We halt, so close he could slap the car's
hood. Instead he snaps to attention,
arm cocked in a crisp salute,
gaze frozen above our heads.

Is he drunk? On drugs? A PTSD-crazed vet
tired of being invisible? My husband waves
him toward the curb. Chin grizzled, spine
rigid, eyes vacant, he holds his ground.

I hold my breath, count heartbeats.
He twitches, whimpers, shakes himself
like a half-drowned stray dragged
from deep water, steps aside.

Will rails at cost-cutters who closed
hospitals, dumped helpless patients
onto the street to fend for themselves.
I think of David, my little brother.

He never learned to speak. Is he a derelict
who frightens strangers on busy streets?
For a time, his fawn's eyes met mine
…then turned inward.

AT LOW EBB

White-fanged winter stalks my house,
lovely and lethal as a wolf on the prowl.

Its frigid breath fogs the windowpanes.
Ice claws the screen door.

Between the back porch
and the woodpile, wind-driven snow

weaves like a vagrant on drugs,
frayed coattails flapping.

Hearts at low ebb, we stoke the fire
and sip mugs of scalding Szechuan tea.

Last April's poems in praise
of peach trees in bloom

and purple lilacs' perfume
ring false as idle promises

scribbled by an absent lover
whose return remains in doubt.

Like a strand of sooty pearls,
pigeons huddle wing to wing

on the swaying lifeline
that links us to the grid.

A dead bird felled from its perch
juts through the drifting snow.

Blue and stiff as frozen fingers,
splayed feathers point skyward.

WHAT SISTERS DO

(for RM)

When you phoned after midnight,
convinced you were about to miscarry,
I promised you, this time

>   your child would be born alive,
>   healthy, at its appointed time.
>   You believed me. She was.

Outside the delivery room a stone-faced
nurse questioned my right to be with you—
Sisters? You don't look like sisters.

>   Blind-sided, I improvised —
>   *It's not my fault I'm adopted!*
>   She stepped aside.

Nestled in the crook of my arm, your new daughter
rooted for a nipple—eyes blue as yours,
contented as if she were mine.

>   Propped up on pillows, bare feet strapped
>   into stirrups, smile bright as surgical lights
>   overhead, you blew me a kiss. *We did it!*

When you lost your sobriety, blamed everyone else,
I refused to give up. You chose men who robbed you,
bullied you, shamed you in public—lied to shield

>   eggshell-brittle pride, ran away. No good-byes,
>   no forwarding address. In time the gaping wound
>   healed over. Today only a faint scar remains.

I still wear the carnelian necklace—
your gift for my forty-fifth birthday,
the scarf—rippling silk, hand-painted

—you bought for me
at a pricey Santa Fe boutique
…because that's what sisters do.

UNHINGED

When they cup my face
your hands say
what you seldom put
into words.
Now they lie limp,
splayed fingers
turn gray. I can't
feel your breath
on my cheek,
find your pulse.

Time comes unhinged—-
a buffalo herd's crazed
stampede, a slug's labored
creep. I kneel beside you
deaf to the siren's shriek.
A stranger's hands grip
my shoulders, pull me
away. Struck by the medics'
portable lightening
your body jolts—once,
twice. *We've got a pulse!
Load him up!*

I climb into the ambulance,
count freeway exits. Decades
reduced to blurred landscapes
glimpsed from a bullet-train.
We limp past mile-markers,
our future on life-support.

I teeter—a glass figurine
in an earthquake—close
my eyes, whisper your name
—a one-word prayer.

HEARTBREAK

Night & day the concentrator pumps oxygen
through the raveled coils of your fifty-foot
hose. Forked prongs prod your nostrils.

Despite opiates you sleep badly.
Beside you I hardly sleep at all.
Your heart thumps, jostles us both.

Womb-dark, our hot nights
know no boundaries, no sound
but the squat machine's murmur,

its slap & suck like wavelets
lapping packed sand at low tide,
wearisome soundtrack of your pain.

Surgeons sliced you open, pried ribs
apart, snipped clogged arteries,
stitched healthy veins in place.

Haunted, I try to forget.
Doubts circle like feral cats
trapped in a dank cellar.

UNWELCOME CHANGES

I welcome change, you say,
when it's my idea.

Change doesn't knock before entering.
It wasn't your idea to lose your hair, your hearing,

to learn, while shooting hoops with your grandsons,
that you've lost your trusty three-point jump shot

from center court. Would you welcome change
if it dulled your razor-edged mind?

I don't welcome my brittle bones, withered skin,
blurry vision, shaky fingers that fumble with my key,

can't hook earrings through my earlobes,
thread a needle. Whose hands are these,

too feeble to lift a teapot, fill a cup
without spilling? Who would I be

if I couldn't tie my own shoes?
If my truth-teller's words went missing?

Without them I'd squint at you, mute as a cat
befuddled by lights and shadows flickering

on a TV screen. I might get lost midway
between bedroom and kitchen,

slip a paring knife into my pocket, hide
my half-drained cup in my underwear drawer.

When I can't recall your name,
forget my own,

leave me.

WAYPOINTS

How to account for my children's
transformation from pudgy infants
to graying grown-ups who hover

and fuss at their fast-growing offspring, fret
over pitfalls that could derail their futures?
How to fathom my own mutation—

from feisty tomboy who leapt out of trees,
scaled fences, sprinted across high-speed
roadways—into this seventy-something *bubbe**

whose shrinking body I no longer recognize,
afraid her frail bones might shatter if she falls?
Relegated to back corners of dark closets

our history's been telescoped into a jumble
of creased black & white snapshots,
Kodachrome slides, a half-century's journals

scrawled in spiral notebooks—all crammed
inside cardboard boxes. I thumb random pages
headed by month, date—no year. Sift through photos

of unfamiliar faces—no names. Who were they?
When and where were these shots were taken?
Did we imagine our fleeting moments

would never fade? That our memories
would stand forever, like a garden filled
with Rodin sculptures cast in bronze?

Now all I have is this paper trail—
waypoints on a path through fog.

* grandmother in Yiddish

4—INFLECTION POINTS

NO VISIBLE SCARS

No one saw my grandmother
shake her chubby toddler, dangle
her like a squirming kitten

from a second story window,
loom over her on the landing,
raised foot aimed at her back.

At school she sat in the last row,
walked home alone. No witness divulged
how cagey fists skirted her moonflower face,

colt-like legs below her hem, bare arms
in warmer weather. She grew taller.
Her mother changed tactics.

Verbal assaults fractured no bones,
veiled threats left no visible scars—
only a skittish fear of heights, spells of vertigo.

Her nightstand held a jumble of sleeping pills,
stimulants, pain pills, anti-depressants.
She shredded our nights with sobs, doors

slammed shut, water glasses hurled
against walls, strings of colorful curses.
By day she berated us often—never beat us.

Twenty years ago her daughters
spread her ashes on a windswept field
spangled with California poppies.

When I cook for friends as she loved to do,
her boisterous laughter fills my kitchen.
In my studio she hums as I shape slim-necked

vases, pregnant pitchers, tea-bowls curved to nestle
in upturned palms. With the gift of her artist's hands,
I press traces of her spirit into my soft red clay.

EMILY'S TEACUP

In the doorway of her retrofitted bedroom
I froze. The machine—big as a capsized
refrigerator—had swallowed her body,

reduced her to a severed head on a pillow.
Her tangled hair trailed like seaweed,
her gaze drifted among ceiling tiles.

When she glimpsed me upside-down
in her tilted mirror, her eyes reeled me in.
I pulled a chair close, made small talk.

Emily's caregiver showed me a bone-china
teacup just painted: violets—
heart-shaped leaves, purple petals.

"I grip… brush… in my teeth…
My helper…lifts… colors…
…the cup."

Will she live out her short life battling for breath?
Painting knickknacks for the church bazaar?
The iron lung creaked like a submarine's pump.

*

For five decades Emily has shadowed me—
dogged me like an unpaid debt, an encrypted
message I've failed to decipher.

Lately, tools slip from my grasp. My left hand
twitches—once docile clay lurches off-course.
Today Emily waltzed into my studio, splendid

in full teenybopper regalia—powder-blue
sweater set, crinolines, bobby socks,
blond pony tail fastened with satin ribbon.

Dusk. I lower the blinds, their cords frayed
like tendons in my hands. In the doorway
I pause and remember Emily's teacup.

ELEGY FOR MY VACUUM CLEANER AND OTHER ARTIFACTS

Hobbled by a broken wheel, it lurched
at my heels like an arthritic terrier.
Its duct-taped snout wheezed, thrust

into corners, burrowed under bookshelves,
probed the crevasse between wall
and antique Larkin secretary desk.

It gobbled up fuzz-balls, cobwebs, flyaway
hairs, mud clods in monsoon season.
Today it whined, stank of scorched metal.

Its death-shriek sent me scrambling to pull
the plug. As a stopgap, we borrowed
my husband's shop vac—industrial grade,

with a jet-engine's roar. The machine sucked up
debris like a tornado. Power-crazed, we moved
furniture frozen in place for decades,

pried away faceplates under our fridge,
our classic 1950's Wedgewood stove.
Like pot-hunters plundering Anasazi ruins,

we unearthed a petrified Christmas cookie,
clay shards dated by glaze, a peach-colored chunk
of Vanderlaan's pricey handblown glass platter—

our housewarming gift to ourselves. I recalled
how the walls shuddered when I slammed
my bedroom door, the gut-wrenching crash

as delicate glass shattered against the brick floor,
and the bitter impasse that triggered my rage.
I tossed the gleaming fragment into the garbage.

Some grievances are best forgotten,
dead fires raked under,
old bones left in the ground.

BIOGRAPHY OF A POMEGRANATE TREE

Sunday mornings, cycling with friends
to a downtown café, I pass a pomegranate
tree—Persian princess in exile,
caged behind a spear-tipped fence.

Every May her flame-red blossoms
dress up the yard's drab gravel, distract
from peeling stucco, a cluttered porch,
cracked window panes.

Pollen-dusted bees careen through her leaves
in a nectar-fueled frenzy. After July's
monsoons, swelling fruit drags
her branches nearly to the ground.

Rust colored pomegranates
ripen slowly, ordinary-looking
as brass doorknobs—no Mardi Gras
colors, no heady fragrance,

no hint of toothsome flesh to tempt
a hungry vagrant. No flash of rubies
under frog-skin, royalty covert
except for the crown-shaped calyx.

I pause by the fence, gauge
the space between bars, distance
to the nearest succulent sphere.
My guilty fingers fall short.

Late November, battered by headwinds,
I notice one stubborn pomegranate
still clings to its storm-stripped branch.
Scattered below, its sisters lie haloed

by dark stains, dregs of sticky purple blood
spilled on parched soil, burst skins
dirt-brown, brittle as sunbaked leather,
husks of last summer's gifts, gone to rot.

ENGLISH AS A SECOND LANGUAGE

At the Downtown Center for Immigrants' Rights
hand-lettered signs are in Spanish. Alien sounds
park at the curb. No plodding iambic pentameter.
No consonants slurred or hard-hitting as Acid Rock.

No silent E's left to dangle at the ends of words—
limp flags on days with no wind. No double consonants
yoked together, inseparable Siamese twins.
No swarms of unpredictable vowels—

flattened O's that sound like A
in "cop," "Constitution," "job," "God."
Clipped, in the second syllable of "custody."
Pronounced like U in "money," "compassion."

In ESL class, English stages a coup.
Bewildered as toddlers, Level One students
strain to recognize words—like trying
to pick out raindrops in a downpour.

They relearn the alphabet—English letters
have different names—break lifelong habits
of lips, teeth, tongue. To make an American R
your tongue mustn't touch the roof of your mouth.

B & V do not sound the same, but *D & T*
often do. *I* is not pronounced *eeee,*
but sometimes the letter *E*
sounds like *I* in Spanish.

Chopping onions, scrubbing skillets, co-workers speak
no English. Hearing your accent, Big Box checkout
clerks grimace, shrug. At your neighborhood
grocery store they nod, say *Buenos días.*

With doctors, at Parent-Teacher conferences,
rely on your kids. TV and movies have subtitles,
but the Citizenship test is given in English.
Register for Level Two.

LA PATRONA

No jobs for fourth-grade drop-outs in Parral, Chihuahua.
Tía Demetria sent bus money—promised,
    Domestic servants always find work in El Paso.

Six days a week I cleaned other people's houses,
mopped kitchen floors, scrubbed toilets,
dusted mahogany tables. Hummed *corridos**

while I polished cooktops, microwave ovens, buffed
patio doors mirror-bright. Each woman I worked for
was *La Patrona*—the Boss-lady, the person in charge.

They taught me to use dishwashers, vacuum cleaners,
washers & driers. I soaked blackened skillets
in vinegar, rubbed out scorch marks with baking soda,

cut greasy build-up with lemon juice
—tricks *abuelita* taught me:
    Poverty's no excuse for a dirty house.

La patrona shook her head, then nodded
when soap-scum dissolved, fingerprints
vanished, copper-clad cookware gleamed.

At Community College I took classes—ESL,
Financial Literacy, Self-Employment Tax Law,
Computer Skills. Passed the citizenship exam,

earned my GED. Seventeen years later I still clean
other people's houses. I provide a valuable service,
set my own terms. *Aquí La Patrona soy yo.*

The Boss-lady here is me.

                                           * corridos: Mexican folk ballads

FINAL WALK-THROUGH

Old hand built adobe houses grow sideways.
Ramón guides the buyers through daisy-chained rooms,
side-steps an old stereo, a knock-kneed card-table stacked
with books, a laundry basket crammed with cook pots,
mixing bowls, wooden spoons, a *molinillo* for whipping
hot chocolate. ...*All this to the dump.*

On the walls white rectangles linger—ghosts
of family photos now gone. The sole memento,
a landscape painting—silver-sequined sky,
rainforest, orchids & ferns, a village asleep
at the foot of a twin-towered church.
Mi pueblo... my home. I sold it. Tomorrow they take it.

Marooned in an empty room, a stripped bed slumps
under suitcases, work clothes, mud-crusted
boots, a tattered Audubon guide.
*All I can take... Old dog put down,
puppy adopted. Neighbor promise
she feed homeless cat.*

He clears a space, sits. *My wife's family built
this house, 1916. We live here since '62.
Planted trees, painted walls, fixed kiva
fireplace, new brick floors. Pero... she died.
five years ago and I... Indocumentado.*
Quicksilver hands fall still.

In the yard he explains how to water the plants,
when to feed and prune his wife's roses.
House clean by Sunday. Se lo prometo.
They shake hands, wish him *Buena suerte.*
Unblinking, the homeless cat waits
for him to fetch kibble, fill her water bowl.

ACTS of FAITH

JANET:

Asked how they're feeling today,
        my students reply,

Muy bien, bendito sea Dios—
        Very well, God be praised.

Any plans for tomorrow? Next week?
        Next year? The rest of their lives?

They temper their American Dream
        with *Si dios quiere…* God willing…

MAGDALENA:

My *barrio* was a war zone.
Crippled by poverty, hassled by *narcos*
and pimps, I scrounged stray cash for the bus
to Nogales, crossed the border on foot—

no papers, no friends, no money, no English.
Nightmares hounded me—stink of gunpowder,
missing neighbors, raped *quinceañeras,*
the mutilated naked corpse of a high-profile reporter.

Still I miss street markets—mangos, papayas,
jícama con chile y limón, roasting corn,
sizzling *tacos al carbón*, shriek of caged parrots,
blare of mariachi brass.

God must have other plans for me.
Perhaps I'll be a teacher like Janet—
help others like me, raise students
instead of children…*si dios quiere…*

ALICIA:

At dawn I spotted the black SUV
on the prowl—engine muffled,
a wolf's growl. I phoned my husband,

escaped through the alley, brought
my five-year-old to my English class.
How could I leave him at Head Start?

If ICE picked me up, they'd put him
in foster care—I'd never see him again.
If my husband's detained

they'll deport him. Tonight, *si dios quiere,*
he'll be safe with *tíos* in Española, but my son
and I need somewhere to stay.

God sees all, knows all, but help comes
when I speak my sorrows only to Him.
He likes to hear it from my lips alone.

JANET:

Compañeros huddle. Hands clasp,
        heads bow, lips mutter prayers.

At nine o'clock they square
        their shoulders, take their seats.

I correct grammar, pronunciation,
        improvise drills to improve

their comprehension,
        build vocabulary,

practice conversation skills—
        my own modest act of faith.

APPLIED SCIENCES

In the aquarium's staged underwater gloom, my breath
fogs the glass. Jostled by spellbound strangers, I watch
sharks circle their tank—truculent, hunger-driven.

Behind me a voice rasps: *Biology's just applied
chemistry—chemistry's applied physics—
physics is applied math. For answers, study Math.*

Dressed in a tweed coat with elbow patches, Math
saunters into my bedroom's pre-dawn hush, briefcase
bulging with data to define faith, analyze art, quantify
love, translate the mystery of consciousness

into statistics. Has Math found the formula
for Leonardo's genius, Wolfgang's inspiration?
Numbers describe how walnut-halves mimic my brain's

wrinkled hemispheres. Spirals recur in nautilus shells,
seahorse tails, fiddlehead ferns, my unruly hair;
in dust devils, hurricanes, DNA's double helix,
in diamond-bright galaxies strewn across indigo skies.

Can numbers explain why? To make sense of the world
I trust tools I can touch—microscopes, telescopes,
slim books packed with mind-bending metaphors
caught in a poet's searchlight gaze.

Mathematics computes the speed of light,
maps the egg-shaped orbits of comets.
Which equation can predict the outcome

of my love-drunk grandson's high stakes
gamble as he shrugs off parental doubts,
discards roadmaps, upends expectations?

LOVE-LOCKS ON THE RIO GRANDE

Clamped to the pedestrian bridge
rusted padlocks rattle, shackles clank
like a dying rez-truck's engine.

Do smitten couples recite vows here, invite
witnesses? Drop keys over the railing
to solemnize their commitment?

Some might hide spares inside a pocket,
a purse. Either partner could memorize
a combination lock's six-digit code, return

on the sly, fling it into the murky flow.
Each lover should keep their own key
like a mutually agreed-upon pre-nup—

it's Albuquerque, not Paris. No ball-room princesses
in gossamer and sequins here. Dust-devils waltz
with updrafts, tumbleweeds ride bucking gusts,

mirages break promises. Stunted by drought,
confounded by weather at odds with the calendar,
dreams wither, romance wanders off-course.

Yet our stubborn fifty-plus year marriage
punched through crusty *caliche*, sank deep roots
in our quarter-acre of bone-dry ground.

On sweltering nights ecstatic coyotes unleash
a mariachi serenade. My vocal chords strain
to keep pace with their trumpets and violins.

Wingbeats thrum October skies—
raucous Canada geese, resonant sandhill
cranes throng our vanishing wetlands.

The Rio Grande's a junction,
not a border—paradox thrives
on both sides. Love-locks belong.

BUSHCRAFT

Moss-carpeted, dew-drenched, soggy
as milk-soaked bread, the ground squishes
under my weight. I wobble, grope for balance.

On a rain-slick slope, loose gravel skids,
sends me sprawling. I land sideways, gash
my right knee, rip my favorite nylon pants.

I'll scrub out these bloodstains, patch
this L-shaped flap, point to it proudly—
merit-badge for a basic lesson in bushcraft.

I re-learn simple things: inch down
wet scree leaning forward, knees
flexed, toes pointed straight ahead.

To support a dodgy ankle
keep boots snug—tighten
laces, tie firm double-knots.

To navigate under an inky sky, memorize
unfamiliar star clusters, follow the moon's
direction, the galaxy's glowing arc.

To spot endangered wildlife, freeze.
Peer past layered foliage to glimpse
iridescent blue-green on a *kereru's* wing,

russet stripes on a saddleback's shoulder.
Note how the *tui* bird's white ruff
trembles before it sings.

Ancient conifers cradle seedlings
till they burst through peeling bark, orchids
and ferns sprout between forked branches.

Like a cat suckling her litter, a fallen *rimu's*
rotting trunk feeds a row of leafy saplings.
I reconsider my aging body's potential.

GRACE

On a bluff above Abiquiu lake,
blue evening holds its breath.

I strain to hear its heartbeat,
scribble detailed notes

about shapes and shadows…
yet the shifting light eludes me.

Summer clouds on the horizon bloom,
break apart and reconvene—

a caravan of nomads, robes ablaze.
Topaz, coral, garnet, amber—

color stains the canyon's craggy walls.
In slanting light, sandstone glows—

a jewel-box in the desert.
Twilight deepens to indigo.

I strive to memorize the way
the lake mirrors the darkening sky,

to weave water and stone
into a song of praise.

Lifeless as stale seeds, my lyrics
fail to sprout. Stillborn melodies fade

like the whistle of a distant train.
Inside my ribs a frantic sparrow flails.

As nightfall wraps me in its rich brocade,
the breeze brushes my arm with a lover's touch.

I hug my knees against the chill, as one by one
faint stars appear like pinpricks through black satin.

ACKNOWLEDGEMENTS

With gratitude to the publications where these poems first appeared:

Sin Fronteras, Writers without Borders
    2016— The Ruins
Poem
    2017— Evidence of an Earlier Life, My Mother's Voice, Unhinged
    2018— At Low Ebb, Provenance
    2020— Migration's Sound Track, Bushcraft
Constellations, A Journal of Poetry and Fiction
    2017— Three Citizens, Cycling in Indian Country
    2018— No Visible Scars, Heartbreak
    2020— Category V, Variations on a Theme, Final Walk-Through
    2021— Unresolved
Passager
    2018— Flashbacks
    2022— Oral History Project
Loch Raven Review
    2020— No One Stays in Honduras, At Night
The Avalon Literary Review
    2020— Elegy for Our Vacuum Cleaner and Other Artifacts
I-70 Review
    2020— Biography of a Pomegranate Tree
The Main Street Rag
    2020— English as a Second Language
San Pedro River Review
    2020— In Lockdown
"Neighbors," a "Crack the Spine" themed Anthology
    2020— Border Town
bosque 9
    2019— Cristina's Odyssey—2019
The MacGuffin
    2021— Applied Sciences, Unwelcome Changes

As a child growing up in Mexico City, **Johanna** shuttled between two languages, two cultures. She began writing early to make sense of her world, and often translated for monolingual people to help them make sense of theirs. The experience made her value clarity of meaning and intent.

Since 1970 Johanna has lived in New Mexico where she and her husband built an adobe home a short walk from the Rio Grande. Together they raised two children and built a successful career as studio potters.

Always happiest outdoors, she takes frequent hikes, bike rides and camping trips throughout the desert Southwest. Visits to the region's archeological sites deepened her ties to the land, its long history and vast landscapes. Place matters—Johanna's chosen place speaks through her poems.

Once retired from studio practice, she put her language skills to work as a volunteer ESL teacher and aide to immigrant families. "Waypoints," a collection of poems written over the past ten years, tells some of their stories as well as her own. Because her life has straddled the border, her work does too.

Between 2014 and 2019, she attended the San Miguel Poetry Week in Mexico where she participated in workshops with Carol Ann Duffy (nine times Poet laureate of the UK), Sir Andrew Motion (also a former UK Poet Laureate), and American poets such as Tony Barnstone, Kevin Young, Jennifer Clement, Thomas Lux and Therese Svoboda.

In 2014 Johanna began publishing in regional and national journals. Recent poems have appeared or are forthcoming in Poem, Passager (Honorable Mention, Poetry Contest 2019), *bosque 9,* Constellations (Pushcart Nominations in 2018 and 2020), Crack the Spine (themed anthology "Neighbors," 2020), The Main Street Rag, The San Pedro River Review, The Lock Raven Review, the MacGuffin, as well as the migration anthology "From Everywhere a Little."

www.ingramcontent.com/pod-product-compliance
Lightning Source LLC
Chambersburg PA
CBHW030224170426
43194CB00007BA/848